Consider
the
Lilies . . .

Treasures of the Vatican Library
(Book Illustration)

Consider
the
Lilies . . .

Turner Publishing, Inc.

ATLANTA

The illustrations in this book are taken from Latin volume 4326
in the Barberini Collection, The Vatican Library.

Published by Turner Publishing, Inc.
A Subsidiary of Turner Broadcasting System, Inc.
1050 Techwood Drive, N.W.
Atlanta, Georgia 30318

First Edition 10 9 8 7 6 5 4 3 2 1
ISBN: 1-57036-102-9

Printed in the U.S.A.

Treasures of the Vatican Library:
Book Illustration

❖

CONSIDER THE LILIES . . ., the first volume in the Treasures of the
Vatican Library series, offers a selection of miniature masterworks of book
illustration from the collections of one of the world's greatest repositories of
classical, medieval, and Renaissance culture. The Vatican Library, for six
hundred years celebrated as a center of learning and a monument to the art
of the book, is, nevertheless, little known to the general public, for
admission to the library traditionally has been restricted to qualified
scholars. Since very few outside the scholarly community have ever been
privileged to examine the magnificent hand-lettered and illuminated
manuscript books in the library's collections, the artwork selected for the
series volumes is all the more poignant, fascinating, and appealing.

Of course, the popes had always maintained a library, but in the fifteenth
century, Pope Nicholas V decided to build an edifice of unrivaled mag-
nificence to house the papacy's growing collections—to serve the entire
"court of Rome," the clerics and scholars associated with the papal palace.
Pope Sixtus IV added to what Nicholas had begun, providing the library with
a suite of beautifully frescoed rooms and furnishing it with heavy wooden

benches, to which the precious works were actually chained. But, most significantly, like the popes who succeeded him, Sixtus added books. By 1455 the library held 1,200 volumes, and a catalogue compiled in 1481 listed 3,500, making it by far the largest collection of books in the Western world.

And the Vatican Library has kept growing: through purchase, commission, donation, and military conquest. Nor did the popes restrict themselves to ecclesiastical subjects. Bibles, theological texts, and commentaries on canon law are here in abundance, to be sure, but so are the Latin and Greek classics that placed the Vatican Library at the very heart of all Renaissance learning. Over the centuries, the library has acquired some of world's most significant collections of literary works, including the Palatine Library of Heidelberg, the Cerulli collection of Persian and Ethiopian manuscripts, the great Renaissance libraries of the Duke of Urbino and of Queen Christiana of Sweden, and the matchless seventeenth-century collections of the Barberini, the Ottoboni, and Chigi. Today the library contains over one million printed books—including eight thousand published during the first fifty years of the printing press—in addition to 150,000 manuscripts and some 100,000 prints. Assiduously collected and carefully preserved over the course of almost six hundred years, these unique works of art and knowledge, ranging from the secular to the profane, are featured in this ongoing series, Treasures of the Vatican Library, for the delectation of lovers of great books and breathtaking works of art.

Consider the lilies,

how they grow:

they neither toil nor spin;

yet I tell you, even Solomon

in all his glory was not

clothed like one of these.

My beloved speaks and says to me:
"Arise, my love, my fair one,
and come away; for now the winter
is past, the rain is over and gone.
The flowers appear on the earth;
the time of singing has come,
and the voice of the turtledove
is heard in our land."

THE SONG OF SOLOMON 2:10-12

Let us crown ourselves

with rosebuds before they wither.

Let none of us fail to share in

our revelry; everywhere let us

leave signs of enjoyment,

because this is our portion,

and this our lot.

They are like trees planted by
streams of water, which yield
their fruit in its season,
and their leaves do not wither.
In all that they do,
they prosper. The wicked
are not so, but are like
chaff that the wind drives away.

For your word went forth,

and at once the work was done.

Immediately fruit came forth

in endless abundance and of

varied appeal to the taste,

and flowers of inimitable color,

and odors of inexpressible fragrance.

These were made on the third day.

2 ESDRAS 6:43–44

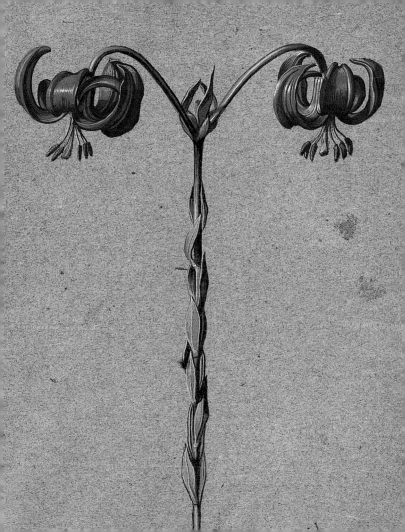

The kiln tests the potter's vessels; so the test of a person is in his conversation. Its fruit discloses the cultivation of a tree; so a person's speech discloses the cultivation of his mind. Do not praise anyone before he speaks, for this is the way people are tested.

ECCLESIASTICUS 27:5–7

And the fading flower of its
glorious beauty, which is on
the head of those bloated with
rich food, will be like a
first-ripe fig before the summer;
whoever sees it, eats it up
as soon as it comes to hand.

As for me, I was like a canal from a river, like a water channel into a garden. I said, "I will water my garden and drench my flower beds." And lo, my canal became a river, and my river a sea. I will again make instruction shine forth like the dawn, and I will make it clear from far away. I will again pour out teaching like prophecy, and leave it to all future generations.

ECCLESIASTICUS 24:30–33

No good tree bears bad fruit, nor
again does a bad tree bear good fruit;
for each tree is known by its own
fruit. Figs are not gathered from
thorns, nor are grapes picked from
a bramble bush. The good person out
of the good treasure of the heart
produces good, and the evil person
out of evil treasure produces evil;
for it is out of the abundance of the
heart that the mouth speaks.

He said to me, "Count up for me those who have not yet come, and gather for me the scattered raindrops, and make the withered flowers bloom again for me; open for me the closed chambers, and bring out for me the winds shut up in them, or show me the picture of a voice; and then I will explain to you the travail that you ask to understand."

ECCLESIASTICUS 5:36–37

A voice says, "Cry out!"

And I said, "What shall I cry?"

All people are grass, their constancy

is like the flower of the field.

The grass withers, the flower fades,

when the breath of the Lord blows

upon it; surely the people are grass.

Let the believer who is lowly
boast in being raised up,
and the rich in being
brought low, because the
rich will disappear like
a flower in the field.

JAMES 1:9–10

Blessed are those who trust in the
Lord, whose trust is the Lord.
They shall be like a tree planted
by water, sending out its roots
by the stream. It shall not fear
when heat comes, and its leaves
shall stay green; in the year of
drought it is not anxious, and
it does not cease to bear fruit.

Your two breasts are like two fawns, twins of a gazelle, that feed among the lilies. Until the day breathes and the shadows flee, I will hasten to the mountain of myrrh and the hill of frankincense. You are altogether beautiful, my love; there is no flaw in you.

Listen to me,

my faithful children,

and blossom like a rose

growing by a

stream of water.

ECCLESIASTICUS 39:13

*Send out fragrance
like incense, and put forth
blossoms like a lily.
Scatter the fragrance,
and sing a hymn of praise;
bless the Lord
for all his works.*

ECCLESIASTICUS 39:14

The earth brought forth
vegetation: plants yielding
seed of every kind,
and trees of every kind
bearing fruit with
the seed in it.
And God saw
that it was good.

I am a rose of Sharon,

a lily of the valleys.

As a lily among brambles,

so is my love among maidens.

I will give you your rains
in their season, and the land
shall yield its produce,
and the trees of the field
shall yield their fruit.
Your threshing shall overtake
the vintage, and the vintage shall
overtake the sowing; you shall eat
your bread to the full, and live
securely in your land.

LEVITICUS 26:4–5

My beloved is mine and

I am his; he pastures his

flock among the lilies.

Until the day breathes

and the shadows flee,

turn, my beloved, be like

a gazelle or a young stag

on the cleft mountains.

And they told him,

"We came to the land

to which you sent us;

it flows with milk

and honey,

and this is its fruit."

As an apple tree among the trees of the wood, so is my beloved among young men. With great delight I sat in his shadow, and his fruit was sweet to my taste. He brought me to the banqueting house, and his intention toward me was love. Sustain me with raisins, refresh me with apples; for I am faint with love.

THE SONG OF SOLOMON 2:3–5

For the sun rises with its
scorching heat and withers
the field; its flower falls,
and its beauty perishes.
It is the same way with
the rich; in the midst of a
busy life, they will wither away.

The fig tree puts forth its figs,

and the vines are in blossom;

they give forth fragrance.

Arise, my love, my fair one,

and come away.

❖

THE SONG OF SOLOMON 2:13

For our allotted time is the passing
of a shadow, and there is no return
from our death, because it is sealed
up and no one turns back.
Come, therefore, let us enjoy the good
things that exist, and make use of
the creation to the full as in youth.
Let us take our fill of costly wine
and perfumes, and let no flower
of spring pass us by.

Why does the way of the guilty prosper? Why do all who are treacherous thrive? You plant them, and they take root; they grow and bring forth fruit; you are near in their mouths yet far from their hearts.

JEREMIAH 12:1–2

Ah, the proud garland of

the drunkards of Ephraim,

and the fading flower of its

glorious beauty, which is

on the head of those

bloated with rich food,

of those overcome with wine!

Woe is me! For I have become

like one who, after the summer

fruit has been gathered,

after the vintage has been gleaned,

finds no cluster to eat;

there is no first-ripe fig

for which I hunger.

As for what fell among the thorns,
these are the ones who hear;
but as they go on their way,
they are choked by the cares and
riches and pleasures of life,
and their fruit does not mature.
But as for that in the good soil,
these are the ones who, when they
hear the word, hold it fast in an
honest and good heart, and bear
fruit with patient endurance.

From the fruit of the mouth one's stomach is satisfied; the yield of the lips brings satisfaction.

These are blemishes on your love-
feasts, while they feast with you
without fear, feeding themselves.
They are waterless clouds carried
along by the winds; autumn trees
without fruit, twice dead, uprooted;
wild waves of the sea, casting up
the foam of their own shame;
wandering stars, for whom the deepest
darkness has been reserved forever.

The fruit for which your soul
longed has gone from you,
and all your dainties and
your splendor are lost to you,
never to be found again!

REVELATION 18:14

How graceful are your
feet in sandals, O queenly maiden!
Your rounded thighs are like jewels,
the work of a master hand.
Your navel is a rounded bowl
that never lacks mixed wine.
Your belly is a heap of wheat,
encircled with lilies.

From your lofty abode you water
the mountains; the earth is satisfied
with the fruit of your work.
You cause the grass to grow for the
cattle, and plants for people to use,
to bring forth food from the earth,
and wine to gladden the human
heart, oil to make the face shine, and
bread to strengthen the human heart.

PSALMS 104:13–15

Death and life are in

the power of the tongue,

and those who love it

will eat its fruits.

But I was like a gentle lamb led to the slaughter. And I did not know it was against me that they devised schemes, saying, "Let us destroy the tree with its fruit, let us cut him off from the land of the living, so that his name will no longer be remembered!"

JEREMIAH 11:19